Made in the USA
Columbia, SC
31 July 2022

64367411R00061